COMPREHENSION SKILLS

SEQUENCE

LEVEL B

Linda Ward Beech

Tara McCarthy

Donna Townsend

STECK-VAUGHN
ELEMENTARY · SECONDARY · ADULT · LIBRARY

A Harcourt Company

www.steck-vaughn.com

Editorial Director:	Diane Schnell
Project Editor:	Anne Souby
Associate Director of Design:	Cynthia Ellis
Design Manager:	Cynthia Hannon
Media Researcher:	Christina Berry
Production:	Rusty Kay
Cover Illustration:	Stephanie Carter
Cover Production:	Alan Klemp
Photograph:	©PhotoDisc

ISBN 0-7398-2630-1

2 3 4 5 6 7 8 9 0   BNG   04 03 02 01

Sequence is about time. It means the order of things. In this book you will look for the sequence of things in a story.

Do you like games? All games are played in a sequence. Look at the picture on this page. What do you think happened before it was taken? What will happen next? What happens at the beginning of your favorite game? What happens last?

What Is Sequence?

Sequence means *time order*. When things happen in a story, they happen in a sequence. Something happens first. Then other things happen. Then something happens last. How can you find the sequence in a story? Just look for clue words, like these:

today	then	Monday
first	after	June

Try It!

Here is a story about apples. See whether you can follow the sequence. Circle all the clue words.

Apples

People have liked apples for many years. But the New World has not always had apple trees. People carried the trees to America about four hundred years ago. At first people planted trees only in the East. Later, travelers carried them west. Now apples grow in most states. We use them in pies and jellies. But most of all, we just like to eat them raw.

How to Find Sequence

Try to follow the sequence in the story about apples. On this page there are two sentences about the story. Write the number **1** on the line by the sentence that tells what happened first. Write the number **2** by the sentence that tells what happened next.

_____ Travelers carried apple trees west.

_____ People planted apple trees in the East.

♦ Read all the words in the two sentences above. Now read the story about apples again. Try to find the words in the two sentences that are in the story. Did you find the words _travelers_ and _East_ in the story? Draw a line under these two words.

♦ After you find the words _travelers_ and _East_, find the clue words that are close by. The clue words that go with _East_ are _at first_. The clue word that goes with _travelers_ is _later_. The clue words tell you how to put things in a sequence. _At first_ tells you that something happened at the very beginning. _Later_ tells you that something happened after something else.

♦ If you still cannot find the sequence, try this. Look at the sentences in the story. One sentence is first. Another sentence is second, and another one is third. The sentences are in order. The action in the first sentence happened first, and the action in the second sentence happened second.

To check your answers, turn to page 60.

Practice with Sequence

Each unit in this book has one story. You will answer questions about the sequence of each story. Read this story about railroads. Answer the question.

◆

Railroads Across America

It was 1862, and it was hard to get from East to West in America. Some people decided to build train tracks across the grasslands of America. One year later, workers began to build the tracks in the East. They laid tracks going toward the West. Two years later, workers in the West laid tracks going toward the East. Six years after the work started, the workers connected the tracks in Utah. Two trains came slowly down the tracks. One was from the East. One was from the West. East and West were joined at last!

Questions

Now answer question 2. Question 1 has been done for you.

_B_ **1.** When did people decide to build railroad tracks?
      A. before 1862
      B. in 1862
      C. after 1864

_____ **2.** When did the workers in the East begin?
      A. before the workers in the West
      B. in early times
      C. in 1862

To check your answers, turn to page 60.

How to Use This Book

In this book there are 25 stories. Read the stories. Think about each question. Write the answer where it belongs.

Check your answers yourself. You can tear out pages 61 and 62. Find the unit you want to check. Fold the answer page on the dotted line to show the right unit. Write the number of answers you got right in the *score* box at the top of the unit page.

Hints for Better Reading

◆ Find words in the questions that are the same as words in the story.

◆ Find the clue words in the story.

◆ Look at the order of the sentences.

Challenge Yourself!

If you are a good reader, try this. Read each story. Cover it with a sheet of paper. Answer the questions without looking at the story.

Writing

On pages 30 and 58, there are stories with questions. These do not have answers for you to choose. Think of an answer. Write it in your own words. On pages 31 and 59, you are asked to write your own story. You are given a prewriting activity to help you. You will find suggested answers on page 60. But your answers may be very different.

Fire!

No family wants its home to catch fire. But it's good to plan for a fire just in case. Talk with your family about what to do if a fire starts. Everyone should have a plan for getting out of the house. Be sure to choose a safe place to meet after everyone gets away from the fire.

What should you do if there is a fire? First let people know about the fire. Yell the word *fire*. Pound on the walls with your hands.

Then feel the door of your room. If the door is warm, don't open it. If it's cool, open it just enough to look out. If you see fire or much smoke, close the door fast.

If you don't see fire or smoke, you can go out the door. Shut the door behind you. That will slow down the fire. Now find a way out. Stay away from the smoke. The air is best near the floor. So it may be safest to crawl when you leave the house.

If you can't leave your room, close your door. Cover the crack under the door with clothing. Then open the window or break the glass with a chair. Crawl out the window carefully. If the window is high off the ground, don't jump! Wave a towel out the window, and yell for help.

When you get out of the house, run to the place you and your family chose to meet.

1. Put these events in the order that they happened. What happened first? Write the number **1** on the line by that sentence. Then write the number **2** by the sentence that tells what happened next.

_____ Yell the word *fire*.

_____ Go to the meeting place you chose.

_____ 2. What do you do first if there is a fire?
  A. break the windows
  B. let people know about the fire
  C. practice what to do in case of fire

_____ 3. When do you open the door?
  A. after you see flames and smoke
  B. while you cover up the windows
  C. after you feel the door to see if it is warm

_____ 4. What should you do when you get out?
  A. wave a towel
  B. meet everybody in a safe place
  C. open the windows

Making Clothes Long Ago

Long ago, clothes weren't bought in stores. Everything was made at home. Here is how people made a wool shirt.

Wool is the hair of sheep. In the spring a family shaved off a sheep's wool. First they pulled dirt and hay out of the wool. Then they washed the wool in lakes or ponds and dried it. Next they rubbed fat into the wool. Then people combed the wool with *wool cards*. These were little boards with metal teeth. The combing formed the wool into neat rolls.

After the wool was combed, the spinner went to work. Usually the mother or sister did this. The spinner made wool thread. She wrapped the finished thread around a piece of wood. Then the family boiled flowers in water to color the wool. They dipped the thread into the colored water. Then someone hung the wool thread to dry. After the threads were dry, a machine called a loom was used to make cloth. The cloth was made using one thread at a time. Each thread went over and under other threads. It took about two miles of thread to make cloth for just one shirt!

At last the cloth was finished. Shirt pieces were cut from the cloth. Then they were sewed together by hand, using needle and thread. Wood or seashells made pretty buttons. Then the shirt was ready to wear.

1. Put these events in the order that they happened. What happened first? Write the number **1** on the line by that sentence. Then write the number **2** by the sentence that tells what happened next.

   _____ The family shaved off the hair of the sheep.

   _____ The spinner went to work.

_____ 2. When was fat rubbed into the wool?
   A. after the wool was washed and dried
   B. after the thread was colored
   C. when the shirt pieces were cut out

_____ 3. When was the wool spun into thread?
   A. before fat was rubbed into it
   B. after it was wrapped around some wood
   C. after it was combed into neat rolls

_____ 4. When did people color the wool?
   A. when the shirt was put together
   B. after the thread was put on a piece of wood
   C. after the thread was made into cloth

Pencil Pick-Up

It was Sunday. Mrs. Sandoval thought of all the things she had to do on her day off. She hurried into the kitchen past the counter. Her elbow bumped the full can of pens and pencils. Crash! They fell in a heap on the floor. Mrs. Sandoval moaned. Her chores would have to wait.

Maritza came when she heard the crash. She saw the pile. She knew what happened. Her mom sat on the floor and reached for a pen. All of a sudden, Maritza saw the mess a new way. "This looks like a game I've played!" she said.

She sat on the floor, too. Then she carefully lifted a pencil off the top of the pile. None of the other pens or pencils moved. She put the pencil in the can. Maritza picked up a pen and another pencil. Her mom watched closely. As Maritza lifted a third pencil, one moved. Her turn had ended. The game looked fun. Her mom leaned down for a try.

Mrs. Sandoval slowly picked up a pen. Nothing moved, so she picked up another. Her turn ended when a pencil moved. Soon all the pens and pencils were back in the can. Mrs. Sandoval smiled. Then she dumped them out. Chores could wait. They played again.

Steck-Vaughn • Comprehension Skills Series

1. Put these events in the order that they happened. What happened first? Write the number **1** on the line by that sentence. Then write the number **2** by the sentence that tells what happened next.

_____ The can of pens and pencils fell.

_____ Mrs. Sandoval hurried into the kitchen.

_____ 2. When did the pens and pencils fall?
   A. after Maritza came into the kitchen
   B. before Mrs. Sandoval moaned
   C. after Mrs. Sandoval picked them up

_____ 3. When did Maritza's turn end in the picking-up game?
   A. before she heard the crash
   B. after a pencil moved
   C. after Mrs. Sandoval leaned down

_____ 4. When did Mrs. Sandoval dump out the pens and pencils?
   A. before she hurried into the kitchen
   B. after she did her chores
   C. after they were back in the can

The Dai Family, Americans

The Dai family had been living in America for five years. One night Mrs. Dai said, "We must talk about something. We left Vietnam in fear. We had to run and hide. At last we came to America. No one tries to hurt us here. Now we have the chance to be Americans. But if we become Americans, we will no longer be Vietnamese. What should we do?" The Dais talked for a long time.

Then Mr. Dai said, "I'm proud that I was born in Vietnam. But the country we loved is not there anymore. We can't go back. It would be good if we became Americans."

One bright Saturday Mr. Dai went to the library and got some books. He asked the children for help. They had been going to school. They helped their parents learn to read English. The Dais read about how Americans choose their President.

Then the Dais took some tests. Next the Dais filled out some papers. People checked the papers. They also checked to make sure the Dais had not broken any laws. After a month the family got a letter from a judge. He wanted to see them on Monday. On that day they put on their best clothes and went to the judge. First the judge asked Mr. and Mrs. Dai if they would follow the laws. They both said they would. Next the judge had them raise their right hands. They said they would be true to America. The judge said, "You are now Americans."

1. Put these events in the order that they happened. What happened first? Write the number **1** on the line by that sentence. Then write the number **2** by the sentence that tells what happened next.

_____ The Dais took some tests.

_____ The Dais filled out papers.

_____ 2. When did Mr. and Mrs. Dai learn to read English?
  A. while they lived in Vietnam
  B. after the judge said they were Americans
  C. before they went to see the judge

_____ 3. When did the judge see the Dais?
  A. on Monday
  B. on Wednesday
  C. one bright Saturday

_____ 4. What did the judge ask the Dais first?
  A. if they would raise their right hands
  B. if they would promise to follow the laws
  C. if they would promise to be true to America

Inventions

Animals can't change their world. People can. They can think of new ways and new things. Some of the first inventions were stone tools and speech. Then people thought of ways to make fire and wheels. Some inventions have failed. Most inventions have been helpful.

In 1913 Garrett A. Morgan fixed sewing machines. One day he saw that polish for the machine needles helped make hair straight! Straight hair was the style. He began the Morgan Hair Refining Company. Business was great.

The polish helped people to style their hair. Another one of Morgan's ideas helped save lives. He invented a gas mask. In 1916 a waterworks tunnel blew up. More than thirty men were trapped in the tunnel. It was filled with poison gas. Morgan was called to help. He and three others put on gas masks. They found the men and carried them to safety. A year later American soldiers used Morgan's gas mask. It kept them safe from harmful gas used in World War I.

In time Morgan grew rich. He was one of the first African Americans in Cleveland to own a car. The car gave Morgan a new thought. He made a three-way traffic light to make the roads safer. Morgan's inventions helped life go well— and stop well, too!

1. Put these events in the order that they happened. What happened first? Write the number **1** on the line by that sentence. Then write the number **2** by the sentence that tells what happened next.

_____ Morgan invented a three-way traffic light.

_____ Morgan owned a car.

_____ 2. What was invented before wheels?
- **A.** gas masks
- **B.** speech
- **C.** sewing machines

_____ 3. When did Morgan start his hair refining company?
- **A.** 1913
- **B.** 1916
- **C.** 1936

_____ 4. When was Morgan called to the tunnel of trapped men?
- **A.** after he made a three-way traffic light
- **B.** after he carried men out
- **C.** after he invented the gas mask

The Ghost Train

It was April 1865. President Lincoln was dead. He had been shot as he watched a play. A long train carried Lincoln's body to its last resting place.

The train started in Washington, D.C. That is where Lincoln had lived while he was President. Black flags flew from the great engine. Many wheels rolled on the rails. Click-clack went the wheels. Click-clack! People waited by the tracks. They cried as they watched the train go by. The train finally stopped in Springfield, Illinois. That was to be Lincoln's last home.

Lincoln died a long time ago. But to this day, some people wait by the train tracks in late April. The people say that on a certain dark night the air grows very still. Then, if there is a moon, a cloud covers it. A large, black engine comes out of the dark night. Black flags wave in the air. The train is as quiet as the wind. The cars and engine seem to float on the tracks. Old-timers say that the train is a ghost train. They say their watches stop while the train goes by.

Steck-Vaughn • Comprehension Skills Series

1. Put these events in the order that they happened. What happened first? Write the number **1** on the line by that sentence. Then write the number **2** by the sentence that tells what happened next.

_____ The air becomes very still.

_____ A black engine comes quietly down the tracks.

_____ 2. When did President Lincoln die?
    A. in May
    B. in 1865
    C. in 1975

_____ 3. Where did the train finally stop?
    A. Springfield, Illinois
    B. Washington, D.C.
    C. the White House

_____ 4. When does the ghost engine come?
    A. before the air becomes very still
    B. before people's watches stop
    C. before clouds cover the moon

King of the Worms

Jody Gerard was ten years old when he decided he needed a job. He thought it might be fun to raise worms. He could sell them to farmers and people who fished. So in the spring, he bought many worms. Jody put the worms in clean dirt. He gave them water, leaves, and corn all summer. The worms got fat, and Jody sold many of them. But that winter he did not put them in a warm place. The cold weather killed all the worms.

The next spring Jody tried again. He bought more worms. He took good care of them. Many people bought Jody's worms. When winter came Jody took the worms inside so they would stay warm.

One day when Jody was 12, he got a letter. It was from the state of New York, where he lived. The letter said, "Everyone who sells things has to pay taxes!" Jody made only 50 cents a day selling worms. But he still had to pay part of that money to the state. Jody told many people in his town what had happened. Soon some people from a television station came to Jody's house. He told them about his problem. They showed a film on TV of their talk with Jody. Many people saw it. The people began to write letters to the state. The letters said that the law was unfair. Finally the law was changed. Children like Jody can now sell things without paying money to the state.

1. Put these events in the order that they happened. What happened first? Write the number **1** on the line by that sentence. Then write the number **2** by the sentence that tells what happened next.

_____ Jody had to pay money to the state.

_____ Television people came to Jody's house.

_____ 2. When did Jody first sell worms?
   A. when he was 10
   B. when he was 14
   C. when he was 12

_____ 3. When did all of Jody's worms die?
   A. in the summer
   B. in the spring
   C. in the winter

_____ 4. When did the state try to get money from Jody?
   A. right after he started selling worms
   B. when he was 12 years old
   C. after the law was changed to help children

A Bag of Toads

Shandra took a paper bag from the shelf. Tyrell had put a beetle on her head this morning. She was going to play a joke on him this evening.

Shandra went to the pond. She searched under logs and in the weeds. Soon she had some toads in her bag. She thought she'd put some in the garden. She'd keep one as a pet. She also needed a nice big toad to put in Tyrell's bed. Shandra grinned to think how he would jump. Then she stopped.

She spied a squirrel with its leg caught in a wire fence. It looked dead, but Shandra saw that it was breathing. She threw her jacket over it and tried to pull the wires apart. They moved a bit. The squirrel's leg slipped out. Shandra picked up her jacket. Soon the squirrel scooted away. Shandra smiled to see him free again.

Shandra heard sounds from the paper bag. The toads were trying to jump. Quickly she spilled them onto the mud. She nodded as they jumped away. Now what kind of joke could she play on Tyrell? She put acorns in her bag. Later she'd hide them in the toes of his shoes.

1. Put these events in the order that they happened. What happened first? Write the number **1** on the line by that sentence. Then write the number **2** by the sentence that tells what happened next.

_____ Shandra searches for toads.

_____ Shandra gets a paper bag.

_____ 2. What did Shandra see after she had some toads in her bag?
   A. a squirrel caught in a fence
   B. a beetle in her purse
   C. her jacket

_____ 3. When did the squirrel scoot away?
   A. after Shandra set the toads free
   B. after Shandra put acorns in her bag
   C. after Shandra picked up her jacket

_____ 4. When did Shandra let the toads go?
   A. before she heard sounds from the bag
   B. before she searched under logs
   C. before she collected acorns

Making a Rose Necklace

Here is how you can make a necklace that smells like roses. First find roses that smell very sweet. Pick about four cups of rose flowers. Pick only the colored flowers. Be sure to keep the green parts out.

Then tear the flowers into very tiny pieces. Put the pieces into a bowl, and add one half of a cup of cold water. Use a wooden spoon to mash the flower bits. Mash them into a smooth paste.

Next cook the rose paste in a big pot. You can use a pot made of glass or iron. Cook the paste on low heat. Watch it all the time. If the paste gets too hot and begins to boil, it will not smell good anymore. Stir the rose paste so it will not burn. The paste is ready when it sticks to the sides of the pot. Turn off the heat, and let the paste cool.

When the paste has cooled, it's time to make rose beads. Squeeze the paste in your hands. It should be stiff and a little sticky. If it's still really wet, pat it with a soft paper towel. Now make little balls about an inch across. Then stick a big needle through each ball to make a hole. After you make the holes, put the beads on clean paper to dry. Drying them will take two or three days. Turn the beads over carefully each day. This helps them dry evenly. When the beads are dry, they are hard and black. Rub them well with a soft cloth to make them shine. Now string the beads on fishing line. The dark beads will smell of roses.

1. Put these events in the order that they happened. What happened first? Write the number **1** on the line by that sentence. Then write the number **2** by the sentence that tells what happened next.

_____ Rub the rose beads with a soft cloth.

_____ String the beads on fishing line.

_____ 2. When do you add water to the rose flowers?
   A. before you pick them
   B. after you tear them into little pieces
   C. after the rose paste is cooked

_____ 3. When do you cook the rose paste?
   A. before making rose beads
   B. after it is stiff
   C. while tearing the flowers into pieces

_____ 4. When do you let the beads dry?
   A. after you put them on a string to wear
   B. after you put the needle through them
   C. before you make the little, round balls

23

A Cowboy's Day

It was a cool spring morning. The cook shouted, "Everyone up! Get your food before I throw it out!" The sleeping cowboys woke up and stretched. They went to the cook's wagon for breakfast.

All winter the cattle had been out in the pasture. They ran wild and ate grass. But now the owners wanted to see how many cattle they had. So the cowboys had to find the cattle and catch them. They called this rounding up the cattle.

After breakfast the men got on their best horses and rode away. Soon they found some cattle. The cowboys rode around the herd. Then they started moving the cattle. The animals were afraid, and some didn't want to go. But the cowboys kept them moving. Finally they got to a big, wooden pen.

Then the cowboys looked at the cattle. Some of the cattle had a mark burned into their hair. The marks showed who owned the cattle. But the young cows didn't have any marks. They had been born just that winter. When a cowboy saw a calf without a mark, he caught it with a rope. He knew who owned the calf because each mother cow had a mark. The calf had to be given the same mark the mother cow had. The cowboys pressed a hot iron into the calf's fur.

Soon all the calves were marked. Late that night the cowboys would have a little party. They would joke, sing, and tell stories.

1. Put these events in the order that they happened. What happened first? Write the number **1** on the line by that sentence. Then write the number **2** by the sentence that tells what happened next.

_____ The men caught calves with a rope.

_____ The cowboys looked at the cattle.

_____ 2. When were the cattle brought to the pen?
     A. after the cowboys found the cattle
     B. when the cook shouted
     C. after the cowboys had a party

_____ 3. When did the cowboys put marks on the cattle?
     A. before they ate breakfast in the morning
     B. when they first found them in the pasture
     C. when the cattle got to the big pen

_____ 4. When did the cowboys have a party?
     A. before all the calves had been marked
     B. late at night
     C. when they ate breakfast

The Missing Person

One day 12 silly people went fishing in a nearby river. There some of the people fished in the water. Others fished on the land. You can guess which ones caught fish. When the sun went down, it was time to go home. Said one man, "This was a fine day! Isn't it wonderful that none of us drowned?" Said another, "Let's count ourselves to be sure."

So each person counted the others. They all forgot to count themselves. They all began to weep. "There are only eleven of us. One of us is gone!"

A peddler heard the people crying. When he found out why, he offered to find the missing person. In return the people would give him all their money. So the peddler began to count the silly people out loud. He gave each person a whack on the back as he counted. He whacked the last person hardest of all. "Here is your missing person!" he cried.

The silly people thanked the peddler and paid him well for finding their missing friend.

1. Put these events in the order that they happened. What happened first? Write the number **1** on the line by that sentence. Then write the number **2** by the sentence that tells what happened next.

   _____ The silly people counted themselves.

   _____ The silly people went fishing.

_____ 2. When was it time to go home?
   - **A.** in the morning
   - **B.** at noon
   - **c.** in the evening

_____ 3. When did the people begin to cry?
   - **A.** after they counted each other
   - **B.** while they were fishing
   - **c.** before the sun went down

_____ 4. When did the peddler count the people?
   - **A.** before he knew why they were crying
   - **B.** after he knew why they were crying
   - **c.** while they were counting each other

The Perfect House

Marta thought their house was too small. She and Victor bumped elbows in the kitchen. They squeezed by in the hall. The front room had space for only two chairs and a television. Still, Victor thought their house was just perfect.

One day the doorbell rang. Cousin Franco and his wife Carmen came to visit. They brought their four boys. While they were there, a delivery man knocked. He asked Marta to keep three crates for Joe Rivas until he got home. The twins came over from next door. They wanted to meet the boys they saw in the window. They set their CD player next to the crates. While the door was open, Eduardo walked by with his dog. It looked like a fiesta in the house. So he said hello and took his dog in. After that Miss Flo came to borrow two eggs.

Marta went to get the eggs. She stepped over the CD player and under someone's arms. Next she climbed around the crates and squeezed between chairs. Then she bumped through the crowd in the kitchen. She almost tripped over the dog. At last she got the eggs back to Miss Flo.

In time the guests said good-bye. Marta spread out her arms. She said, "This house seems so big!" Victor thought it was just perfect. Marta agreed.

1. Put these events in the order that they happened. What happened first? Write the number **1** on the line by that sentence. Then write the number **2** by the sentence that tells what happened next.

_____ The twins came to visit Marta.

_____ Marta stepped over the CD player.

_____ **2.** How did Marta feel about the house before the guests came?
  A. that the house was too small
  B. that the house was just perfect
  C. that the house was so big

_____ **3.** Who were the first guests?
  A. the twins
  B. a delivery man
  C. Cousin Franco and his family

_____ **4.** When did Marta bump through the crowd in the kitchen?
  A. before Miss Flo asked to borrow eggs
  B. before Marta almost tripped
  C. before Marta squeezed between chairs

Writing

Read the story below. Think about the sequence, or time order. Answer the questions in complete sentences.

Julio was making a bowl out of clay. First he took the clay out of the bag. Then he rolled it flat. Next he shaped it into a bowl. He let it dry. Last he baked it. He had a nice bowl for a gift.

1. What did Julio do first?

_____

_____

2. What did Julio do after he made the clay flat?

_____

_____

3. What did Julio do before he baked the bowl?

_____

_____

To check your answers, turn to page 60.

Prewriting

Think about something that you have done, such as planting a garden, catching a fish, or washing a dog. Write the events in sequence below.

> What I Did

> First

> Next

> Last

On Your Own

Now use another sheet of paper to write a story about what you have done. Write the events in the order that they happened. Use time order words.

To check your answers, turn to page 60.

Help! I Can't Swim!

What if you fall out of a boat and can't swim? Don't get scared. Remember, your body is full of air. Learn to bounce in the water. Bouncing can save your life.

First take a deep breath and hold it. Then stand up in the water. You really can float standing up. The water will cover your eyes, but the top of your head should stick out. Let your arms and legs hang loose. Put your chin on your chest.

Stay under the water until you need a breath. Then bounce out of the water to get one. Bouncing is very easy to do. Bring your arms up in front of you, with your hands facing down. Keep them just under the top of the water. Then bring up one leg. Pretend you're trying to walk. Now push your hands down and step. After you do this, your head will come out of the water. Blow out all your air, and shout for help.

Now take a breath of air and hold it. Let yourself slip under the water again. Let your arms and legs hang loose. When you need more air, bounce up again. Keep doing this until people come to help you.

Anyone can learn bouncing. It doesn't take long to learn. The man who thought of bouncing shows it to little children. Bouncing is easy. And it has saved many lives.

1. Put these events in the order that they happened. What happened first? Write the number **1** on the line by that sentence. Then write the number **2** by the sentence that tells what happened next.

_____ Bring your arms up in front of you.

_____ Blow out all your air, and shout for help.

_____ **2.** What do you do first to bounce in the water?
    A. hold your breath and stand up in the water
    B. look around and shout for help
    c. bring your hands up in front of you

_____ **3.** What do you do next?
    A. bounce out of the water and take a breath
    B. hold your breath
    c. dive into the water head first

_____ **4.** What do you do after that?
    A. look for something to float on
    B. swim towards the land
    c. take a deep breath and slip back under the water

Stunt Car Driving

A thief runs from the bank. He jumps into a waiting car and roars off. People run after him, but it's too late. He's gotten away. Or has he? Look! Another car is coming toward the thief. The car is not stopping. Crash!!! Suddenly the two cars are in flames. There's been a terrible accident.

Scenes like this in movies thrill people all the time. The accident looks real, but no one is really hurt. These scenes are done by actors called stunt people. They take the place of the regular actors in the dangerous parts.

A director hires stunt people to appear in a film. First the stunt people plan what will happen. This is called rigging the gag. They go over each part of the scene many times. The timing is very important. It may take many days to plan a stunt. The stunt people then check all the equipment. Everything must be in perfect working order.

Then it's time to begin. For a crash scene, the stunt people get into the cars. The cameras roll. At the moment of the crash, the two drivers jump from the cars. The stunt drivers are quick, and their escape does not show on the film.

The shells of two other cars are then towed to the scene. These shells look just like the cars that crashed. Dummy drivers are put into the cars. When the cars hit a trigger in the road, they burst into flames. These shells have no engines and they burn without exploding. The camera takes pictures of it all.

1. Put these events in the order that they happened. What happened first? Write the number **1** on the line by that sentence. Then write the number **2** by the sentence that tells what happened next.

_____ The thief jumped into a car.

_____ The thief ran from the bank.

_____ 2. When do the stunt people rig the gag?
    A. before they do the stunt
    B. as they get in the cars
    C. at the moment of the crash

_____ 3. When do stunt people check the equipment?
    A. after the shells arrive
    B. when they do the stunt
    C. after they plan the stunt

_____ 4. When do the stunt people jump out of the cars?
    A. before they check the equipment
    B. during the crash
    C. after the shells are towed into place

Growing Tiny Popcorn

When Shelly Hoff was eight, a woman gave her three ears of popcorn. They were the smallest ears that Shelly had ever seen. They were about three inches long. That's about half as big as an ear of common corn.

Shelly wanted to grow popcorn. She took some of the seeds from the corn ears. When spring came she dug her garden. Then she put the corn seeds in water for one night. The next day she planted her corn. She put the seeds about one inch under the dirt.

Shelly watered her garden all summer. But she had made one mistake. She had planted the small popcorn too close to some common corn. Her new plants just grew big ears of corn.

The next year Shelly tried again. But this time she made sure there wasn't any common corn nearby. The seeds came up, and the corn looked good. But it didn't grow very fast. Her friends told her that corn is a hungry plant. It takes a lot of food out of the ground. So she put special food on the plants. That fall she picked a few ears of popcorn.

When spring came again, Shelly planted lots of popcorn. The corn had sun, food, and water all summer. By fall she had many small ears of corn.

Now Shelly sells her corn to flower shops. Farmers' markets and gift shops also buy it. She uses her corn money for clothes. She also saves money so she can go to school.

Steck-Vaughn • Comprehension Skills Series

1. Put these events in the order that they happened. What happened first? Write the number **1** on the line by that sentence. Then write the number **2** by the sentence that tells what happened next.

_____ Shelly's plants grew big ears of corn.

_____ Shelly planted corn seeds.

_____ 2. When did a woman give popcorn to Shelly?
   A. when Shelly was 8
   B. when Shelly was 3
   C. when Shelly was 18

_____ 3. When did Shelly put the seeds in water?
   A. before she put the seeds in the ground
   B. after she planted the seeds in the garden
   C. right before she sold the popcorn

_____ 4. What mistake did Shelly make the first year?
   A. planting too much popcorn
   B. not giving the popcorn enough food
   C. planting the popcorn too close to common corn

A Secret King

A king wanted to see what his people were really like. So he put on rags and went for a walk. After a while he got tired and hungry. But when he asked people for food, they laughed and threw rocks at him. They did not know who the poor man was.

Then the king came to an old house. A poor old man and woman lived there. They asked the king to eat with them. They didn't know he was the king. They just wanted to help a tired, hungry man. The woman made a fire. Then she brought cool water for the king to drink. While she was doing this, the old man went outside. He picked some food from the tiny garden. Then he tried to catch a chicken for supper. But the chicken ran fast, and the old man was tired. So he chose some eggs instead.

The woman cooked supper for them. When the food was ready, she put it on the table. The king was given the best food. Suddenly there was a knock at the door. The old woman opened it and saw some neighbors.

"Great King, forgive us," they said. "We threw rocks because we did not recognize you." The king was angry. "I was tired and hungry. You gave me only rocks and bad words. Get out of here!" he shouted.

The poor man and woman were afraid. The king was used to nice food, but they had given him only bread and eggs. The king said, "You gave me the best you had. Because you were kind, I will give money and food to you for the rest of your lives."

1. Put these events in the order that they happened. What happened first? Write the number **1** on the line by that sentence. Then write the number **2** by the sentence that tells what happened next.

_____ The man and woman asked the king to dinner.

_____ The king put on rags and went for a walk.

_____ 2. When did the people of the town throw rocks?
   A. after the king stopped at the old house
   B. when the king asked them for food
   C. when the king shouted "Get out of here!"

_____ 3. When did the old man get the food for supper?
   A. while the old woman made the fire
   B. before the people threw rocks
   C. after the neighbors knocked at the door

_____ 4. When did the woman give the king water?
   A. before he dressed in rags and went walking
   B. after the neighbors came by the house
   C. after she made a fire to cook supper

Coming to America

"Anton sent a letter from America!" Mrs. Novak cried. "Stan, will you read it to us?" Stan read the letter. It said: "I have found work that pays well. I have meat three times a week. But I miss you. Here is money to pay for Stan to come over. He and I will work hard and save our money. Then you, my dear parents, can come. With great love and hope, Anton."

The next day Mrs. Novak put Stan's clothes in a bag. She put bread, cheese, and dry meat in a basket. Mr. Novak said, "Go with our blessing. Love your new land. But do not forget Poland." Then Stan walked the thirty miles to the sea.

At last Stan got on a big boat. He did not have much money, so he stayed in a large room with many people. People slept on shelves. There were no beds. It was very crowded, and it smelled bad. Sometimes high waves made the boat rock. Sometimes Stan got sick from the rocking. The trip lasted six long weeks. One cloudy day someone shouted, "Land! We are here at last!" Stan ran to look. Some people were so happy they cried.

The boat came to an island. Then people got off and stood in long lines. Doctors looked at them to see if they were healthy. Other people asked many questions. They asked, "Have you broken laws? Can you work?" At last Stan was sent to a small boat that took him off the island and to the mainland. Then Stan began the walk to Anton's home and to his new life.

1. Put these events in the order that they happened.
   What happened first? Write the number **1** on the
   line by that sentence. Then write the number **2**
   by the sentence that tells what happened next.

   _____ Stan Novak got on the boat in Poland.

   _____ Anton Novak wrote to his family in Poland.

_____ 2. When did Stan Novak walk thirty miles?
   A. after he got to America
   B. after he got sick on the boat
   C. before he got to the big boat

_____ 3. When did people ask Stan many questions?
   A. before his family got the letter
   B. before he got on the big boat
   C. after he landed on the island

_____ 4. When did Stan walk to Anton's home?
   A. before people asked him many questions
   B. after a small boat took him off of the island
   C. during the long boat trip on the sea

Rip Van Winkle

One day Rip Van Winkle went hunting. He stayed in the mountains all day. Just as he was starting home, someone called his name. He was afraid. He thought he was alone. But he followed the sound.

Soon he met a little old man. The man asked him to carry a small barrel. Rip and the old man walked for a long time. On the way they met some people who were bowling. Rip poured some water from the barrel for everyone. It smelled funny, but he was very thirsty. So he poured some for himself. After he took a drink, he felt very strange. All at once he fell asleep.

When Rip woke up, no one was around. His new gun was dirty and worn out. He thought the strange people were playing a trick. "They took my gun and left me this old one," Rip thought. But he picked it up and went home. When he got to the town, everyone laughed, "Look at those funny old clothes!" they said.

Then Rip walked through the town. There were new houses he'd never seen before. Nothing was the same. He couldn't find people he knew. So he stopped and asked about his friends. Most of them were dead. A few had moved away years ago. "Doesn't anyone know Rip Van Winkle?" he cried. The people looked at him. "Yes, I knew him," said one old man. "Why, you are Rip! But where have you been for twenty years?" he asked. Rip told everyone about the strange mountain people. At first they thought he was telling a joke. Finally they believed Rip had slept the whole time. Rip never went back into the mountains again.

1. Put these events in the order that they happened. What happened first? Write the number **1** on the line by that sentence. Then write the number **2** by the sentence that tells what happened next.

_____ Everyone laughed at Rip's clothes.

_____ Rip stopped and asked about his friends.

_____ 2. When did Rip carry the barrel of water?
   A. after he met the people who were bowling
   B. before he went into the mountains one day
   C. after he met the little old man

_____ 3. When did he meet the people who were bowling?
   A. before he went hunting one morning
   B. after he walked with the little old man
   C. after he slept for twenty years

_____ 4. When did Rip fall asleep?
   A. after he took a drink from the barrel
   B. before he heard someone call his name
   C. after he saw that his hunting gun was dirty

The Brothers Grimm

You know who Snow White is. You've heard of Hansel and Gretel. But have you heard of the Brothers Grimm? If not for them, you might never have heard these tales.

Jakob and Wilhelm Grimm were the oldest of six children. Jakob was born in 1785. Wilhelm was born the next year. They were the best of friends. The brothers lived and worked together for most of their lives.

In 1798 the Grimms moved to the town of Cassel. There they finished school. Then they found jobs in the king's library. Both men loved old stories. In their free time, they searched for old folktales and songs.

From 1807 to 1814, Jakob and Wilhelm collected tales from everyone they knew. Marie Muller was a nanny. She told them the tales of Snow White, Little Red Riding Hood, and Sleeping Beauty. One day the Grimms met Frau Viehmann. She came to their house many times. She drank coffee and ate rolls. She told the Grimms more than twenty tales. Cinderella was one of them.

In 1812 the Grimms' first book of fairy tales was published. The Grimms had meant the stories for grown-ups. They were surprised when children loved them, too. They wanted to find more tales. This time it was much easier. Now people would bring stories to them. The next book of tales was published in 1815. The last book of *Grimm's Fairy Tales* was published in 1857.

1. Put these events in the order that they happened. What happened first? Write the number **1** on the line by that sentence. Then write the number **2** by the sentence that tells what happened next.

_____ The brothers finished school.

_____ The brothers collected tales.

_____ 2. When was Wilhelm Grimm born?
   A. the year before Jakob was born
   B. in 1785
   C. the year after Jakob was born

_____ 3. When did the brothers collect tales from friends?
   A. from 1807 to 1814
   B. in 1798
   C. when they were children

_____ 4. When was the Grimms' first book of fairy tales published?
   A. when the brothers were in school
   B. after they began working in the library
   C. from 1807 to 1814

The Great White Bear

In some languages they are called snow bears or ice bears. We call them polar bears. These giants live in the arctic lands of the far north. Only a few creatures are strong enough to live in such a cold, empty place. Polar bears live alone except when a mother bear has cubs. Female bears have cubs every three years. Like most bears, they are good mothers.

Polar bears mate in April. In September the female goes back to the place she was born. She looks for a den. In December the mother gives birth to two cubs. The cubs are smaller than human babies. And they are just as helpless.

By March the cubs weigh 25 pounds. It is time for them to see the world. They leave the den. At first they are cold and puzzled. They slip and slide as they try to walk on the ice.

Later in the spring, the mother leads the cubs to the seashore. They must catch seals before the ice melts and the seals leave. The cubs walk in their mother's tracks. She teaches them to sniff the air for food. Polar bears can smell food as far as ten miles away.

When they arrive at the seashore, she teaches them how to catch seals. She shows them how to swim in the icy water. When they are two years old, the cubs leave their mother. She has taught them everything they need to know to live on their own.

1. Put these events in the order that they happened. What happened first? Write the number **1** on the line by that sentence. Then write the number **2** by the sentence that tells what happened next.

_____ The mother and cubs stay in the den until March.

_____ The female bear returns to the place she was born.

_____ 2. When do polar bears mate?
   A. usually in April
   B. when they are two years old
   C. in September

_____ 3. When are the cubs born?
   A. later in the spring
   B. in December
   C. when the mother arrives at the seashore

_____ 4. When do the cubs leave their mother?
   A. when they come out of the den
   B. when they are three months old
   C. after they learn to catch seals

Mule Deer

Mule deer are a type of deer that live in western North America. They are known for the strange way they run. They push off the ground with all four feet at once, much like a jackrabbit. Some mule deer live in thick woods on mountains. Others live in dry, empty deserts. Some live near the West Coast. Although they can live in many places, mule deer don't like to live near people.

Mule deer are beautiful animals. They are named for their big, soft, mule-like ears. In the summer the deer are reddish-brown. In the winter they are grayish-brown. They change their coats in the spring and fall. In this way they blend in with the colors of the trees and grass around them.

Male deer, or bucks, grow antlers each year. The antlers begin to grow in April or May. At first they are soft and velvety. They grow through the summer and stop in September. Then the velvet is shed. There is hard bone beneath. In February the antlers fall off. Most antlers have four points. They can grow to be more than two feet long.

A mule deer eats early in the morning and just before the sun sets. The deer must eat quickly. When it is out in the open, it is in danger from its enemies. It chews the grass only enough for it to be swallowed. Then it goes to a more sheltered place. There it can relax.

1. Put these events in the order that they happened. What happened first? Write the number **1** on the line by that sentence. Then write the number **2** by the sentence that tells what happened next.

_____ In February the antlers fall off.

_____ The antlers are soft and velvety.

_____ **2.** When is the deer's coat reddish-brown?
　　　A. when the deer is one year old
　　　B. in the spring and the fall
　　　C. during the summer

_____ **3.** How often do bucks grow antlers?
　　　A. each year
　　　B. every two years
　　　C. only once

_____ **4.** When is the velvet shed from the antlers?
　　　A. when the antlers begin to grow
　　　B. during the winter
　　　C. after the antlers stop growing

Elephants

Elephants are the largest mammals on land. Long ago there were elephants in most countries. Now elephants live only in Africa and Asia. They are smart animals that live together and help each other.

Female elephants live in close family groups. The group is made of mothers and their babies. The young males stay with this group until they are about 14 years old. Then they leave to join a group of male elephants. The males travel in groups, but they are not as close as the family groups. Males often move from one herd to another.

A herd wakes up at four in the morning. The elephants want to start grazing before it gets too hot. They walk to a water hole and drink. The herd walks and eats about 16 hours a day. They eat grass, leaves, bark, and fruit. Sometimes they stop and take naps. At midnight the herd stops for the night. All the elephants lie down and sleep. Some of them snore.

Babies can be born at any time of the year. A baby weighs 250 pounds when it is born. It stands up 15 minutes after it's born. The herd moves slowly for the first few days. The young one walks between its mother and another female. If it gets tired, they hold it up with their trunks. By the third day, the baby can keep up with the herd. At first the little one doesn't know how to use its trunk. Sometimes it steps on it. Sometimes it even sucks its trunk like a human baby sucks its thumb.

Steck-Vaughn • Comprehension Skills Series

1. Put these events in the order that they happened. What happened first? Write the number **1** on the line by that sentence. Then write the number **2** by the sentence that tells what happened next.

_____ Elephants live only in Africa and Asia.

_____ Elephants lived in most countries.

_____ **2.** When do young males join a male herd?
    A. when they are about 14
    B. in the early morning
    C. when their mothers tell them to

_____ **3.** When does a herd wake up?
    A. after it gets hot
    B. at midnight
    C. about four in the morning

_____ **4.** When are baby elephants born?
    A. in the spring
    B. during any season
    C. usually in the summer

Paper

Paper has been around for a long time. It was invented by the Chinese about A.D. 105. In the 1400s the printing press was invented in Europe. For the first time, large numbers of books could be made. Many paper mills were built.

Now we use paper for lots of things. Most of the paper goods we take for granted haven't been in use for very long. One hundred years ago, there were no paper towels or tissues. Paper bags were rarely used. Children in school wrote on slates, not on paper.

Each person in a rich country uses about 350 pounds of paper a year! A person in a poor country uses about 40 pounds a year. This adds up to a lot of paper and a lot of trees! It takes more than two tons of wood to make one ton of paper. The more paper we use, the more trees have to be cut down. Luckily, many kinds of paper can be reused. Egg cartons and newspapers are now made from recycled paper.

Let's take a look at how paper is made. First, of course, the trees are cut down. The logs are carried by truck to a pulp mill. Pulp mills are often built near rivers. It takes a lot of water to make paper. The bark is cut off the logs. Then the logs are rolled into water and ground into chips. Chemicals are added, and the chips become pulp. The pulp is poured onto a moving screen. Water drains out of the pulp. A thin sheet of fibers is left. This sheet is heated and dried. Then it passes through rollers. At last it is paper!

1. Put these events in the order that they happened. What happened first? Write the number **1** on the line by that sentence. Then write the number **2** by the sentence that tells what happened next.

_____ Large numbers of books could be made.

_____ The printing press was invented.

_____ **2.** When was paper invented?
A. in the 1400s
B. one hundred years ago
C. before the printing press

_____ **3.** When is the bark cut off the logs?
A. before the logs are rolled into water
B. after the chemicals are added
C. when a thin sheet of fibers is left

_____ **4.** When is the pulp poured onto a moving screen?
A. when the sheet passes through rollers
B. after the chips become pulp
C. before egg cartons are recycled

Goldfish

If you had traveled in China one thousand years ago, you would have seen many strange sights. But one sight might have really shocked you. Goldfish! The Chinese had begun to keep goldfish as pets, just as you might now. Later the fish were taken from China to Japan. In the 1700s some of these fish were taken to Europe. One hundred years later, they became popular pets in the United States.

These fish can be large or small. If a goldfish is in a small tank, it will grow to be just a few inches long. But if it is placed in a large pond, it will start growing again. It might grow to be 18 inches long! Goldfish are related to large, brown fish called carp.

All goldfish are not alike. You may think of gold or orange when you think of a goldfish. But these fish come in many colors. Some are black. Some are blue. Some have spots. Some goldfish have strange eyes and heads. Bubble-eyes are one rare type of goldfish. Hugh pouches puff out from their eyes. Another strange fish is the lionhead. It has a large, red head. There are more than one hundred kinds of goldfish.

Steck-Vaughn • Comprehension Skills Series

1. Put these events in the order that they happened. What happened first? Write the number **1** on the line by that sentence. Then write the number **2** by the sentence that tells what happened next.

_____ Goldfish were pets in China.

_____ Goldfish were taken to Japan.

_____ 2. When were goldfish first kept as pets?
   A. one hundred years ago
   B. one thousand years ago
   C. in the 1700s

_____ 3. When were goldfish taken to Europe?
   A. after they were taken to Japan
   B. one thousand years ago
   C. before the 1700s

_____ 4. When did goldfish become popular in the United States?
   A. before they were taken to Japan
   B. in the 1700s
   C. one hundred years after they were brought to Europe

Bath Time

Old paintings show that people took baths more than three thousand years ago. Romans set up pipes. They ran saltwater from the sea to a bath house with many rooms. First a bather exercised to get hot. Then the person went into a room to sweat. In the next room, the person got an oil rub. The third room was for a hot bath. The fourth was for a cool rinse. In the last room, the person jumped into an ice-cold pool.

One thousand years ago, a bather in Finland would sit in a wood hut. First the bather threw water onto hot rocks in the hut. It made steam. That made the bather sweat. This was called a sauna. Next the bather was soaped and rubbed. Then the person was hit with soft twigs and rinsed. The bath came to an end with a jump into the snow or a cold stream.

Bath times changed. Five hundred years ago, people began to think bathing was harmful. They used perfume to hide their bad smell. In time they learned that baths were good for their health. American families warmed water in the kitchen. They poured pots of hot water in a tub. Then they took turns to wash. The water got cold before the last one bathed.

Now there are bathrooms with hot and cold water. The water runs through pipes to a tub. What a nice way to take a bath!

1. Put these events in the order that they happened. What happened first? Write the number **1** on the line by that sentence. Then write the number **2** by the sentence that tells what happened next.

_____ American families warmed water in the kitchen.

_____ Bathers in Finland made a sauna.

_____ 2. What did a Roman bather do first?
   A. get an oil rub
   B. exercise to get hot
   C. fill a tub with pots of water

_____ 3. What was the last thing a bather in Finland did?
   A. jump into the snow
   B. get hit with soft twigs
   C. throw water on hot rocks

_____ 4. When did people think taking baths was harmful?
   A. five hundred years ago
   B. one thousand years ago
   C. more than three thousand years ago

Writing

Read the story below. Think about the sequence, or time order. Answer the questions in complete sentences.

> Asha and Keisha went to the pond. They found some frog's eggs. They took some home with pond water and pond weed. They put them into a fish tank. After a week, the eggs started to hatch. "Look!" said Asha. "They're tadpoles!" The tadpoles grew quickly. In seven weeks, they grew back legs. Then they grew front legs. Their tails got shorter. The tadpoles looked more and more like frogs. Their tails went away. The tadpoles had turned into frogs! Asha and Keisha took the frogs to the pond.

1. When did the frog eggs start to hatch?

_____

_____

2. When did the tadpoles grow back legs?

_____

_____

3. When did the tadpoles grow front legs?

_____

_____

To check your answers, turn to page 60.

Steck-Vaughn • Comprehension Skills Series

Prewriting

Think about something that you have done, such as making a sandwich, setting up a tent, or making your bed. Write the events in sequence below.

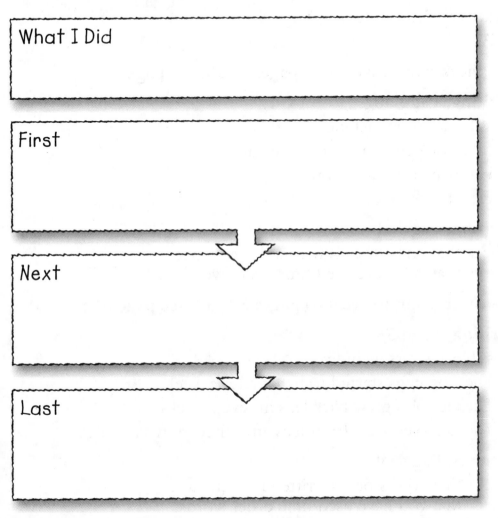

What I Did

First

Next

Last

On Your Own

Now use another sheet of paper to write a story about what you have done. Write the events in the order that they happened. Use time order words.

To check your answers, turn to page 60.

Check Yourself

How to Find Sequence, Page 3
2
1

Practice with Sequence, Page 4
2. A

To check your answers to pages 6–29, see page 61.

Writing, Page 30
Possible answers include:
1. Julio took the clay out of the bag.
2. He shaped it into a bowl.
3. He let it dry.

Writing, Page 31
Check that your story is written in sequence.
Check that you have used time order words.

To check your answers to pages 32–57, see page 62.

Writing, Page 58
Possible answers include:
1. The frog eggs started to hatch after a week.
2. The tadpoles grew back legs in seven weeks.
3. The tadpoles grew front legs after they grew back legs.

Writing, Page 59
Check that your story is written in sequence.
Check that you have used time order words.

Steck-Vaughn • Comprehension Skills Series

Check Yourself

Unit 1	Unit 2	Unit 3	Unit 4	Unit 5	Unit 6	Unit 7	Unit 8	Unit 9	Unit 10	Unit 11	Unit 12
pp. 6–7	pp. 8–9	pp. 10–11	pp. 12–13	pp. 14–15	pp. 16–17	pp. 18–19	pp. 20–21	pp. 22–23	pp. 24–25	pp. 26–27	pp. 28–29
1. 1 2	**1.** 1 2	**1.** 2 1	**1.** 1 2	**1.** 2 1	**1.** 1 2	**1.** 1 2	**1.** 2 1	**1.** 1 2	**1.** 2 1	**1.** 2 1	**1.** 1 2
2. B	**2.** A	**2.** B	**2.** C	**2.** B	**2.** B	**2.** A	**2.** A	**2.** B	**2.** A	**2.** C	**2.** A
3. C	**3.** C	**3.** B	**3.** A	**3.** A	**3.** A	**3.** C	**3.** C	**3.** A	**3.** C	**3.** A	**3.** C
4. B	**4.** B	**4.** C	**4.** B	**4.** C	**4.** B	**4.** B	**4.** C	**4.** B	**4.** B	**4.** B	**4.** B

Sequence • Level B

	Unit 13 pp. 32–33	Unit 14 pp. 34–35	Unit 15 pp. 36–37	Unit 16 pp. 38–39	Unit 17 pp. 40–41	Unit 18 pp. 42–43	Unit 19 pp. 44–45	Unit 20 pp. 46–47	Unit 21 pp. 48–49	Unit 22 pp. 50–51	Unit 23 pp. 52–53	Unit 24 pp. 54–55	Unit 25 pp. 56–57
1.	1 2	2 1	2 1	2 1	2 1	1 2	1 2	2 1	2 1	2 1	2 1	1 2	2 1
2.	A	A	A	B	C	C	C	A	C	A	C	B	B
3.	A	C	A	A	C	B	A	B	A	C	A	A	A
4.	C	B	C	C	B	A	B	C	C	B	B	C	A